Dead Men Don't Talk

by

Catherine Forde

Illustrated by John Kelly

First published in 2009 in Great Britain by
Barrington Stoke Ltd
18 Walker St, Edinburgh, EH3 7LP

www.barringtonstoke.co.uk

ISBN: 978-1-84299-638-6

Printed in Great Britain by Bell & Bain Ltd

A Note from the Author

I live in an old house and one of the bedrooms has a panel of wood cut into the ceiling. There are two holes in the panel. They look like eyes. You can push the panel up to get into the loft. But I don't want to go into the loft. No thanks!

Something lives up there.

It runs about the loft at night and wakes me.

One night, when the 'thing' in the loft woke me, and I couldn't get back to sleep, I began to think about what the thing might be ...

To my big boys

Contents

Chapter 1

Getting My Own Way

"Right. I'll have this room."

This is what I tell Mum the first time I see the new house. Well, it's an old house. But it's new to us.

"I want this room. It's the biggest. OK?" I tell Mum again. Louder.

Then I tell Mum's boyfriend the same thing.

His name's Sam.

And I hate him.

Hate how he's always touching Mum. Snogging her in front of me. Right now Sam's standing with his arm round Mum. It's like he's scared she'll run away.

"This is my room, OK?" I look at Sam. Hard.

Then I tell Jen. She's my sister. Another pain. I'm sick of her. And Mum. And Sam. That's why I want this room. I don't care if it's thick with dust. I don't care if the windows are cracked and dirty. And I don't even care if it smells like something died in here.

I want it.

This room sits at the top of the house. On its own. There's a lav off it. And a shower. A key in the door. Means I can lock myself in. I can move my stuff up here and no one will bother me.

Not Mum. Not Jen. Not Sam.

I won't have to look at Mum and Sam hugging and snogging.

"Oh, Alan," says Mum. She's talking to me now. I'm Alan.

Mum's still trying to make me change my mind about the room. She's looking from me to Sam. All upset. Sam's trying to keep his mouth zipped shut.

He's bursting to tell me to behave.

"Show some respect," he says at last. "You know how hard life has been for your Mum. Don't make things worse."

That's the sort of crap Sam gives out to make me shape up. To make me feel bad.

"Just do what your mum asks for once.
Stop thinking about yourself all the time –"
Sam can't stop himself blurting.

"Don't tell *me* what to do," I yell right
back at him.

But before I can add "You're not my *dad*!"
Mum cuts in.

"This room's *far* too big for one person,
Alan," Mum says. "It's so dark. And there's
no heating. Brrr! It's feels like no one's slept
up here for years. And look at that hatch to

the loft. There's a big hole in it. God knows what's living up there!"

When Mum points up I see this square shape cut out of the ceiling. It has a panel of wood over it. You slide this across so you can get into the space under the roof. The panel of wood's all rot. And black stains. There are two circles cut in the middle of it. They look like a pair of blank eyes staring down.

"Let me and Sam sleep here," Mum nods. "You and Jen have the rooms downstairs. They're fresh and bright."

"Yeah, Alan. This room's creepy," Jen chips in. She likes to keep Mum happy. Jen says it's time Mum was happy again after everything that's happened to her.

Boo hoo!

I couldn't care less. It wasn't Mum who died.

She's still here.

Hip-to-hip with her new boyfriend.

"It feels spooky," Jen adds. "Like it's haunted." She's looking up at the hatch as if she can hear something. And she's frowning. Jen watches far too much crap telly. Next she'll be telling me she hears spirit voices.

"Haunted? Rubbish!" I give Jen a shove.

"Moron," I tell her. Well, she is.

But I'm not Jen, and I NEVER agree with anything Mum says any more. So I snap, "Look, Mum, you made me move in with you and Sam. At least you can give me the room I want. I don't give a shit if it's haunted."

Chapter 2

Looking After Number One

It's a few hours later. I've been down to Sam's transit van and I've dug out all my gear – desk. Computer. Telly. Clothes. I've carted everything up all the stairs. Even my bed. Well, I wasn't going to help Sam and Mum unpack all the IKEA junk they'd bought for their new love-nest. I wasn't sorting out where their bed was going. Sod that.

No. From now on I'm looking after Number One. That's me! Yes. I'm looking after Number One and keeping to myself till I get a job and a flat. Then I'll get myself out of here!

"But first things first," I say out loud and I lift two photos in frames out a shoe-box.

... *thing's firssssstt* ... As soon as I speak, my words echo round about me.

Brrr.

Bit creepy that!

... ings firsssssstt ...

There it goes again. The echo swirls round me as I take off the bubble-wrap I stuck round the photos before we left my old house. First – me and Dad. Standing side by side. Big grins for the camera. Before Dad got sick. We're holding up our fishing rods and a giant trout.

"Best day's fishing in my life," Dad told everyone when he showed them the picture. We never let on the trout was a fake. Made of rubber. Dad loved to wind people up.

My second photo is one Mum hid in a drawer after Dad … after Dad's … when he …

Mum said we all looked too happy in it.

It's the four of us. Christmas Day. Two years ago. We're all cracking up in the photo. Mum, Dad, Jen, me.

"Sing Jingle Bells like Elvis," Dad said while my Gran took the photo.

"... just like Elvis."

Now get this – I'm on my own in this room, right? Dusting Dad's photo-frame with my sleeve. I'm looking into his face. Just wishing, wishing, wishing he could come back. Even for five minutes.

Then suddenly the words Dad said in the photo start to echo. I don't mean inside my head. I mean round the bedroom. It's like a wind picks them up and blows them.

"... just like Elvissssss."

I know it's crazy. Photos don't talk. Dead men don't talk either. But I hear the echo of Dad's voice.

Nah. Must have been me, I tell myself. But I know it wasn't. The echo is so loud, so weird, and lasts so long, I freak. Put Dad's picture down. Turn round slowly. That's when – OK I know this is even more crazy –

but I get this feeling:

Someone's near.

Watching me.

Staring.

Trying to wind me up.

"Jen?" I spin around fast in case she's

come up to see me.

"Quit," I snarl, but I know it can't be Jen. My door's locked. And she wouldn't dare wind me up. I'd lamp her.

"... *ennnn.*" The echo whispers back. Sounds like a deeper voice than Jen's: "... *eeeeennnnnnn.*"

"Mum? Sam?" I turn back into the room and stare into every corner. No one's there.

"*uuuuuuuuuummmmm.*"

This time the echo lasts longer than ever. And when I try to work out where it's coming from, it seems like it's above me. Coming from that hatch.

When I peer up, the echo stops. Dead. Like it's been switched off. Like someone's playing a joke on me, pretending to be a ghost. In my new room everything's so still I feel like I have to hold my breath. In the silence, I hear the clatter of dishes downstairs. Sam singing. Jen joining in. Mum laughing. She sounds miles away. They all do. It's like they belong to another world.

Then, just above my head, from inside the loft, I hear a scrape. A scuff. And footsteps. Like someone in slippers. Pad, pad, padding. But so heavy it makes the ceiling creak.

"Hello?" I whisper. I peer at the hatch. I look hard at the two holes in it. The holes like eyes. A shadow has just passed across them. I swear. The holes look like they've blinked.

Shit. What's up there? I'm thinking as I back my way across the room. Unlock the door.

"A bird?" I say. I feel braver now I'm in the hall. "A rat? A squirrel? Yeah. Something's trapped up there."

I'm talking out loud again, but this time, no echo comes back to me. But I do hear something.

Inside my room as I lock the door.

I hear someone laughing.

Chapter 3

No Thanks

When I come into the kitchen, Jen is at the cooker.

"There's a rat or something in my loft ..." I start to tell her.

I'm not talking to make chit-chat. These days Jen and I never chat unless I want something. And right now I'm only telling Jen about the noise in my loft so she can blab to Sam. That means I won't have to ask him for help. Superman Sam can check out the loft for me. Kill what's up there. Nail the hatch shut. Then go away again and leave me in peace.

"... Yeah. A rat or something bigger. It's in my loft —" I go on, but before I get any further and tell her it's a happy rat, Jen beams out a big smile.

"Hey, I'm making pasta. And a welcome cake. It's a treat for Mum and Sam coz this is their first night in their new house. A new start for Mum," Jen says.

Then she asks me to set the table.

"Piss off," I tell Jen.

There's no sign of Mum or Sam but I can hear their voices. Sam's low. Mum's giggly.

What does Mum find to say to Sam? What does she SEE in him? It bugs me so much I nearly ask Jen –

Why does the sound of Mum's laugh make me feel so mad? So mean? So sad?

Twice as sad as when Mum cried night after night for Dad ...

"Hey, Alan. I'm talking to you," Jen waves her wooden spoon in front of my face.

"Cheer up. You're miles away," she laughs. "I'm asking if you've changed your mind yet?"

"About what?" I snap. Then I grab Jen's wrist so she'll stop flapping her spoon about.

"Your room," Jen stops smiling. "You've made your point. Now let Mum and Sam have the big room. Be kind. The one they're in is tiny. Plus it's next to mine. They need a bit of ... y'know ..."

Jen turns back to the cooker. She goes very red in the face.

I knock the wooden spoon out her hand.

"Shut it. *'Mum and Sam need a bit of 'y'know,"* I copy Jen in a girly voice. "What the hell's 'y'know'?" I go on. Though I know fine well what she means.

I just want her to tell me so I'll think of Dad. Even though it hurts me like a kick in the nuts. At least that means one of his family is still thinking of him. Still missing him. When everyone else has moved on.

"Sam and Mum are just starting out living together," Jen goes on. "And they don't want us to see them all lovey-dovey –"

"I don't want to see that. That's why I need a room as far away as I can get," I butt in. "And I'm not eating any of that shit you're making either."

I grab a loaf, a knife, a jar of peanut butter, and a six-pack of Sam's beer. I leave the kitchen, and I still want to tell Jen some more about the noises in my loft.

But I can't. Can't talk to her. Brother to sister. I have to snap. Snarl. Hurt her. That's just the way things are since Dad died.

"And you can stop whispering into my keyhole too," I shout back at her. "If you know what's good for you."

"What are you talking about? The keyhole to your bedroom? Alan? Wait –" Jen calls after me, but I'm running upstairs. And I don't answer. I want to lock myself in my room before Sam takes his paws off my Mum and pays me one of his man-to-man visits.

"Listen, Alan. Let's be grown-up for a change, buddy," he'll start off.

Before he talks me into moving out of my
room.

Chapter 4

Spot the Difference

I go back into my room and I lock the door. This time I notice how dark it is. I have to feel around the walls till I can find a light switch. The light I turn on comes from a bare bulb dangling down. The glow it gives off is so weak it makes my room look darker. Sick. Yellow.

The wallpaper looks grim.

The corners are full of ugly shadows.

And all my stuff seems to have changed shape since I went downstairs.

My bed is humpy. Like there's someone in it.

My computer sits like a giant head on my desk.

My dressing-gown droops down outside the wardrobe like a Death cloak.

Here I am. In the door-way. With my peanut butter and my beer. I don't feel like eating any more.

I don't want to eat up here, I'm thinking as I look round the room. I don't even want to move into the room or move far from the door. Not when I notice a few things. Things that have changed since I came back upstairs ...

First of all, the room's really cold. Like there's a window wide open. Blowing a gale. And it's a winter night. Freezing outside.

But it's not a winter night. Not now. It's spring. But in my bedroom, the chill's so bad it makes me shiver. Or maybe I'm shivering because I notice the loft hatch is open. Wide open. A great, big, black, gaping hole.

"How did that ...?" I start to say.

My mouth has never been so dry. When I try to say something, my voice scrapes my throat.

"Hel–hello?" I whisper at last. But I don't budge from the door.

41

Are you kidding? I think to myself.

I can hear someone, or some*thing* moving up there. Making the ceiling creak and groan.

A man's voice laughing softly. Tutting.

I stay put. Stare at the hole in the loft. My right hand shuts tight around the knife I brought up with me from the kitchen. My left hand shuts tight round the key to my room. I jab it at the keyhole. I'm trying to fit the key into the lock.

Click. Click. Click.

The noise of the metal key on the wood of the door rings around the bedroom. In the dim, grim light of the room I can't work out where the keyhole is.

Downstairs I hear Jen's voice calling,

"Mum. Sam. Food."

"Fantastic!" Sam's voice shouts back from the hall.

So it's not Sam in the loft. Laughing to himself. Now I push at the door. I'm in a panic.

I grab the handle. Rattle it. Try to find the lock again. Drop the key. Hear it tumble away from me.

"Shit."

I crouch down to look for the key and drop all the food and drink I'm still holding. On hands and knees I grope the floor. I'm bent over, low down, small, and I get the strongest feeling yet that I'm being watched.

From above.

And I know I'm being watched when I feel under my bed for the key and pull out a photo in a frame instead. It's the one of me and Dad. Side by side. Fishing rods. Rubber trout.

Only there's something about the photo that looks different from when I last saw it. I swear me and Dad are standing closer than

I remember. Not just side by side. But our arms are round each other.

"How did ...?"

I'm on my feet. I'm looking at the shelf where I put my photo. Both of my photos. Where I left them.

The shelf's bare.

"Where's the other photo?" I gasp as a big, loud laugh drifts from the hatch.

And that's the moment I really freak.

"Let me out of here, please. I don't want this room any more."

I yelp.

My hands scratch and scrabble the floor.
My knees scrape and slide. I sound like a
bird or a bat or a rat or a squirrel trapped in
a loft.

Only I'm not trapped. When I tug the
door I locked, it opens.

I'm free.

Chapter 5

A Laugh and a Lesson

Two weeks after he moves into the big bedroom with Mum, and I move down next to Jen, Sam goes into the loft with a ladder.

I don't. I'll never go near that room again. Sam and Mum are welcome to it.

It's Jen who tells me that Sam got rid of the old panel in the hatch when he painted the bedroom. He's made a new one to go up there instead.

"But he checked out the loft first. Said there was no sign of life. No droppings. No animals," Jen says. "Just this."

She comes into my room and hands me the framed photo that Sam found in the loft.

It's the happy one that made Mum sad.

Our family – Mum. Dad. Me. Jen. Singing like Elvis.

The one that went missing. When I moved all my stuff downstairs I never found that photo.

Sam told Jen it was lying up in the loft just by the old hatch.

"Well," Jen takes the photo back. She sets it on my telly. "If you want me to believe you, and you REALLY didn't chuck it in the loft, then finding this in our new house must be a sign."

Jen taps her finger-nail on Dad's face.

"Dad's letting us know he's cool. About Mum and Sam. He wants her to be happy."

"You talk crap." I push Jen. Not hard. Just so she falls onto my bed.

You're wrong. I'm thinking.

Dad was teaching me a lesson, wasn't he? About being selfish and mean. You were

having a laugh too. Playing a trick. I smile at Dad's photo while Jen clonks me with a pillow. And maybe it's just the way the sun catches the glass of the frame. But I swear when I look into Dad's eyes, one of them winks back.

Barrington Stoke would like to thank all its readers for commenting on the manuscript before publication and in particular:

Liliana Billing
Josh Burt
Lauren Campbell
Perry Capeling
Kelly Dawson
Grace Dobinson
Justin Grant-Smith
Shellby Grayson
Ben Hancock
Daniel Kelly
Alwyn Martin
Melissa McCabe
Sean McCandless
Deirdre McConnell
Shauna McGreevy

Claire McKieown
Rebekah McRobbie
Lynn McVeigh
Sarah Millar
Billie Mills
Ryan Mitchell
Denise Murphy
Sarah Louise Murray
Toniette Pardoe
Jay Pettitt
Ryan Price
Joanne Shepherd
Andy Shipley
David Shrigley
James Yates

Become a Consultant!

Would you like to give us feedback on our titles before they are published? Contact us at the email address below – we'd love to hear from you!

info@barringtonstoke.co.uk
www.barringtonstoke.co.uk